Up, Up . . . Elephant!

by Alex Eeles
illustrated by Alan Rogers

CAMBRIDGE
UNIVERSITY PRESS

Institute of Education

Sim lived in the rainforest.

Every day, she went exploring
to see what she could see.

But today, something was different.

She could hear a loud noise.

An enormous elephant was standing beside Sim's favourite pool. He was crying.

'What's the matter?' Sim asked.

'I'm too big,' the elephant sobbed.
'My friends can't climb up
onto my back to have a ride.'

Sim had an idea.

'Wait here,' she said, and off she ran.

Sim came back with a lily pad.

'Let's try this,' she said.

boing

6

Sim bounced on the lily pad.

'Here I come!' she said.

She flew through the air ... and into the pool!

'That didn't work,' said the elephant.

Sim had another idea.

'Wait here,' she said, and off she ran.

This time, she came back
with some reeds from the river.

Sim used the reeds to make a ladder.

She leaned it against the elephant and began to climb.

The ladder tickled the elephant's ribs and he laughed.

The ladder wobbled.

Sim fell off and landed on the ground with a bump!

'And **that** didn't work,'
said the elephant.

Sim looked at him and thought.

'Hold out your trunk,' she said.

Sim stepped onto the elephant's trunk and walked along it.

Past his tusks, between his eyes, over his head.

Up, up, and onto his back.

'That worked!' the elephant cried.
'Thank you!

You can be first to have a ride.'

The elephant started to walk with Sim on his back.

Sim smiled.

She had never explored the rainforest like this before!

Up, Up . . . Elephant! Alex Eeles

Teaching notes written by Sue Bodman and Glen Franklin

Using this book

Developing reading comprehension

Sim comes across an elephant with a problem. She tries a variety of ways to help problem-solve until finally, she finds a way that the elephant can give rides to his friends. Sim's reward is a bird's eye view of the rainforest, as she gets the first ride. This story uses a traditional tale story structure of repeated episodes with resolution on the third repetition, but uses natural language patterns to present the conversation between Sim and the elephant.

Grammar and sentence structure

- Use of contractions in direct speech ('I'm'; 'What's'; 'can't'; 'didn't'; 'Let's').
- Adverbial words and phrases ('Every day'; 'This time') express the time elements of the story.

Word meaning and spelling

- Multisyllabic words ('enormous'; 'exploring'; 'favourite') require children to identify parts of words when solving
- Synonyms for talking together convey the characters' feelings more precisely ('asked'; 'sobbed'; 'laughed').

Curriculum links

Geography – Sim gets an aerial view of the rainforest. The children could look at aerial views of their locality available on Google Earth and create maps and images of a familiar place when viewed from above.

Science and Nature – In this story, Sim uses the elephant's trunk to get onto his back. But what is an elephant's trunk really for? Explore this using non-fiction books and websites. The investigations could result in a piece of non-fiction writing.

Learning Outcomes

Children can:

- track accurately across multiple lines of print without pointing
- solve new words by identifying known chunks with words, whilst attending to context and grammar
- discuss character motive and explain reasons for actions.

A guided reading lesson

Book Introduction

Give each child a copy of the book. Read the blurb together. Ask the children to predict what the book will be about and to say whether they think it is fiction or non-fiction, giving reasons and evidence from the text.

Orientation

Give a brief overview of the book: *In this book, Sim comes across an enormous elephant whilst she is out for her daily walk. The elephant is very upset. Let's find out why.*

Preparation

Page 3: Point out the word *'enormous'* and read it, isolating the three separate parts e/nor/mous. Check children know what this means, using the picture to help.

Page 4: Say: *Look for the part where the elephant tells Sim why he is crying. Read it and tell me in your own words. How do we know that the elephant is still crying? Look for a word that helps us understand that the elephant is very sad. Well done, yes, 'sobbed'.*

Page 5: Increase familiarity with the literary phrase *'and off she ran'* by first reading aloud, asking the children to locate it in the text and then rehearsing it.